Life As Seen THROUGH the Eyes of a Poet

Willie J. Pless III

Copyright © 2011

by Willie J. Pless III 25010-Ples

ISBN: Softcover 978-0-984-02600-5

All rights reserved. No part of this book may be reproduced or transmitted in any form by any means, electronic or mechanical, including photocopying, recording, or by any information storage or retrieval system, without permission in writing from the Publisher.

This book was printed in the United States of America

To order additional copies of this book, contact:

Unique Euphony Publishing Group

706-577-3197

www.uniqueeuphony.com

inquiries@uniqueeuphony.com

Edited by Barbara M. Pierce
Cover Design by Kirk Knox

Willie J. Pless III

Dedication

I would like to dedicate my book of poetry to; My wife Jacque who is my all, my children that I love so much, my daughter Valerie Hepburn, the eldest who is dear to me, my son Anthony Pless who I am so proud of, My daughter Deon McIntyre who is my little girl, and my son Bruce Smith (Skeeter) who is my boy. My grandchildren, a gift from God; Anthony Pless Jr.(Man), Andrea Pless, Justin Pless (Jus), Mylan Milwood, Amara Milwood(Mara), Bruce Smith III(Tre), Nicolas Hepburn(Nikko), and Bryce Smith

Special Recognition to; My sister Angela Scott (Nita) and Deidra Roberts (DeeDee), my sister-in-law Elaine Wooden(Auntie Lane) My brother-in-law Phillip Johnson and my mother-in-law Mary Johnson(Ms. Johnson) who all are assisting in my well being through this illness.

Willie J. Pless III

Content

A letter to God   7
God is in Control   8
My God   9
The World Today   10
My Life   11
Putting God on Hold   13
My Guiding Light   15
Don't Wait Until It's Too Late   17
Our Closest Friend   19
Do Your Best   20
Give Life Your Best Shot   21
The Road to God   23
Born Again   25
The Father I Never Had   28
My Daddy   30
A Mother Love   34
My Wife   37
My Darling Daughter   39
The World Today   46
The Answer to Your Prayer   51
Train Your Children   52

Willie J. Pless III

Content

Don't Worry   54
A Real Friend   56

Troubles   59
Sorrow   61
Faith   63
Sickness   65
Love   67
Children   68
Heaven   71
Trust   73
Peace   75
Life   77

One Day at a Time   80
A Broken Heart   82
The Road of Life   83
Hard Times   86

About The Poet   89

Willie J. Pless III

The Pless Family

Willie J. Pless III

A Letter to GOD

Dear Heavenly Father

I don't know where to start

Let me begin by saying

Lord, how great thou art

As I count my many blessings

It's very plain to see

the mercy and the kindness

You've bestowed on me

and as I go about my way

I'll try with all my heart

to help others understand

Lord, how great thou art

Willie J. Pless III

God Is In Control

Have you ever made a plan
that didn't quite work out
did it make you wonder
what it was all about

Life is full of disappointments
It's not only you
We all make plans every day
Sometimes they don't go through

Although there is a reason
That we may not understand
We must rely on God above
And place them in his hand

And if your plan is his will
He will make it so
Put your plan in God's hand
And remember, you must let go

Willie J. Pless III

My God

As I gaze upon the heavens
And behold the stars above

My heart is filled with joy and song
knowing I have God's love

He is always with me
never leaves me alone

And when this life is over
I'll have a heavenly home

'Til then my duty is very clear
I must serve him every day

And spread the news of his love
to others along the way

Willie J. Pless III

The World Today 13
(Life Yesterday and Today)

I look around this world today

And this is what I see

Wars, disasters, crime, hate

And immorality

How much longer can this go on?

I ask myself each day

Things aren't getting any better

Will we find a way?

I pray to God every night

In hope that there will be

A change in this evil world of ours

And peace for you and me

Willie J. Pless III

My Life

I lived what I call a good life
Though my early years were hard
I'm thankful to my family
But most of all to God

I'd like for people to know
I tried my very best
To be on good terms with everyone
I let God handle the rest

God gave me what I asked of him
He didn't hold anything back
And when I strayed off the right road
He put me back on track

I trusted God, he heard my prayers
He answered every one
It wasn't always the way I wanted
But the job was done

Willie J. Pless III

When my days on earth are over
And I'm finally laid to rest
I'll be very satisfied
Knowing I did my best

Willie J. Pless III

Putting God on Hold…
How Dare You!

Just a little longer Lord,
Before I come to you
You see I haven't really done
Some things I'd like to do

Just a little longer Lord
I'd like to have some fun
I think I'll live it up a while
And see you when I'm done

I think there's something wrong today
I don't feel so well
I had to see the doctor
Because my health's begun to fail

Lord, is there something you can do?
This pain I cannot stand
I will give anything
For a touch of your healing hand

Willie J. Pless III

Thank you Lord for healing me
And now that I am well
To those I meet along the way
My story I will tell

Willie J. Pless III

My Guiding Light
Fire at 504 Boulevard

We go to bed each night
After day is done
Expecting to awake again
To see the rising sun

Many will see another day
Some won't make it through
We never know if we will be
In the unfortunate few

There is one very important thing
That we must understand
If we truly believe in God
We'll make it to the Promised Land

God has given us the freedom to choose
And understand wrong from right
I have chosen to follow God
He is my guiding light

Willie J. Pless III

Pless' Aunt Helen

Willie J. Pless III

Don't Wait Until It's Too Late

We stroll along the path of life
Taking it all in stride
Suddenly trouble comes our way
And shatters our selfish pride

The hand of death could strike anytime
You may not have time to pray
If you haven't accepted Christ as your Lord
Why not do it today?

Have you atoned for your sins?
Have you come to Christ?
Please don't wait until it's too late
Or you'll pay the ultimate price

God showed us how much he cares
When Christ died on the cross
He shed his precious blood for us

Willie J. Pless III

That our souls won't be lost

He gave me a second chance to live
My heart and soul to him I give
and I rejoice each time I pray
knowing I'll be with my Lord one day

Willie J. Pless III

Our Closet Friend

God is our father
He knows our every care
no matter when we call on him
God is always there

He sent his son to pay for our sins
which proves that he's our closest friend
He came to earth and cleared the way
for us to be with him someday

I thank God and I give him praise
I'll worship and serve him the rest of my days
and when my life on earth shall end
I'll be with my father and closest friend

Willie J. Pless III

Do Your Best

All of my life I've tried to do
the things that God wants me to

Like resisting temptation to cheat or steal
and never considering to rob or kill

Always to lend a helping hand
when, how and whatever I can

To make a friend here and there
doing my best to love and care

God touched my heart and I've try to do
all of the things he wants me to

And when I'm finally laid to rest
he will know that I did my best

Willie J. Pless III

Give Life Your Best Shot

I lived what I call a good life
Though my early years were hard
I'm thankful to my family
But most of all to God

I'd like for people to know
I tried my very best
To be on good terms with everyone
I let God handle the rest

God gave me what I asked of him
He didn't hold anything back
And when I strayed off the right road
He put me back on track

I trusted God, he heard my prayers
He answered every one
It wasn't always the way I wanted
But the job was done

Willie J. Pless III

When my days on earth are over
And I'm finally laid to rest
I'll be very satisfied
Knowing I did my best

Pless and his Sister

Willie J. Pless III

The Road to God

We travel many roads in life
But no matter where we've trod
There is a very special path
The one that leads to God

This world is filled with troubles
And each of us has his share
Life can bring such misery
'til it seems impossible to bear

Jesus is our savior
And faith is the key
He will work your problems out
Just as he does for me

Trouble comes in many forms
Each day brings something new
Take your troubles to the Lord
He'll work them out for you

Willie J. Pless III

My friend, the choice is yours to make

what will you have it be

A life of peace with God one day

or torment for eternity?

There's one thing we can be sure of

this road is the only way

to have peace and happiness

with Jesus Christ some day

Willie J. Pless III

Born Again

We stroll along the path of life

but do we stop to think?

our lives could end at anytime

It could happen in a blink

Have you atoned for your sins?

Have you come to Christ?

Do not wait until it's too late

or you'll pay the ultimate price

The hand of death could strike anytime

You may not have time to pray

If you haven't come to Christ by now

why not come today?

Willie J. Pless III

He showed his love

When he died on the cross

He shed his blood

That our souls won't be lost

He gave me a second chance to live

My heart and soul to him I give

I sincerely ask, as I pray

To see my Lord and Savior some day

Willie J. Pless III

Pless' Father (Center)

Harvey Lee, Willie James Pless II, William Roosevelt

Willie J. Pless III

The Father I Never Had

A father should be the head of the home

A man that deserves respect

He should be there with his family

To love, provide and protect

Every home should have a father

It wasn't true in my case

He left one day and never returned

Not even to show his face

I never knew the reason

But it made me very sad

To be completely abandoned

By the man I called my dad

Willie J. Pless III

Today I'm proud and happy

And I must confess

Having a family of my own

Has brought me happiness

I've tried to be a good husband

And I've tried to be a good dad

I've tried to be for my children

The father I never had

Willie J. Pless III

My Daddy

When I was just a little boy

With not much food to eat

My clothes were all ragged

No shoes on my feet

Where were you dad?

I went to school in my ragged clothes

Winter came

And I almost froze

When Christmas came

I had no toys

Nor decent clothes like the rest of the boys

Where were you dad?

Willie J. Pless III

I looked for you but you weren't there

It seemed as if you just didn't care

Although my early days were hard,

I thank God for getting me through.

He gave me all the support I needed

That should have come from you

WHERE WERE YOU DAD?

Willie J. Pless III

Willie J. Pless III (Mother)

Willie J. Pless III

Willie J. Pless (Mother)

Willie J. Pless III

A Mother's Love

A mother's love for her children

Is like no other love on earth

She nurtures her children and comforts them

It all begins at birth

Everyone has a mother

I had a special one

I was proud to call her "Mother Dear"

And happy to be her son

Whenever I went to visit

We laughed and talked a while

As I look back on those times

I can see her cheerful smile

Willie J. Pless III

As her days got shorter

She advised me to prepare

As if she had a feeling

She would no longer be there

I miss you darling mother

I hope and I pray

When I come to the end of the road

Well laugh again some day

Willie J. Pless III

Pless' wife

Willie J. Pless III

My Wife

There's a very special person

Who's become a part of my life

She's someone that I appreciate

And proudly call my wife

She's there when I am weary

Supports me in every way

I depend on her love quite often

Just to make it through the day

She's my lover and my companion

I will cherish her to the end

She's also my advisor

And best of all, my friend

Willie J. Pless III

Pless' Daughter & Grandson

Willie J. Pless III

My Darling Daughter

A father's love for his daughter

Is more than words can say

It's a very special bond

That nothing can take away

She can bring joy and laughter

Hopefully, not many tears

A father's love grows and grows

With the passing years

Then comes the day when he must let go

She steps out into the world

Life will take her here and there

But she'll always be daddy's little girl

Willie J. Pless III

Pless' Daughter

Willie J. Pless III

Pless' Son and Grandsons

Willie J. Pless III

Anthony & Valerie

(Pless' son and daughter)

Willie J. Pless III

Pless' uncle & sister

Willie J. Pless III

Pless' Mother & Aunt Helen (sisters)

Willie J. Pless III

Pless' Grandmother, Mattie Bell

Willie J. Pless III

The World Today

I look around this world today

And this what I see

Wars, disasters, crime, hate

And immorality

How much longer can this go on?

I ask myself each day

Things aren't getting any better

Will we find a way?

I pray to God every night

And hope that there will be

A change in this evil world of ours

And hope for you and me

Willie J. Pless III

Each day I wake up searching

Looking all around

The one thing that I'm searching for

Is nowhere to be found

I ask myself this question

Just where can it be?

I'm searching for the answer

but it doesn't come to me

Can it be that hard to find?

Is it anywhere?

To think that it really doesn't exist

Is more than I can bear

I'm looking for something called ***peace***

Willie J. Pless III

And now I can see

If it really doesn't exist

Then it must begin with me

Now that I have an answer

At least that's a start

But it's no good, unless it's understood

That we all must do our part

Can there be peace in this world today?

Can we all get along?

Is there a way of coming together?

Or to create a world that's strong?

In this world divided

And our nation that's falling apart

Willie J. Pless III

We disagree on so many things

How and where do we start?

There's abortion, religion and gun control

Just to name a few

Kids are killing kids each day

Tell me what can I do?

I pray to God for this world of ours

I don't know how long it can stand

There's also the threat of a nuclear war

That could start with the wave of a hand

I believe and trust in God

And I sincerely pray

That no matter what the future holds

Willie J. Pless III

I'll be with him one day

Willie J. Pless III

The Answer to Your Prayer

There comes a time in our lives

When we don't know where to turn

Nor find the help we so desperately need

No matter how much we yearn

Remember there is a God above

He'll hear whenever you call

He'll pick you up when you are down

Even catch you before you fall

There is no task too great for him

And no request too small

Put all of your faith and trust in God

He is the master to all

Willie J. Pless III

Train Your Children

It's hard for our children to understand

why parents always reprimand

We always find a reason to fuss

while getting children to earn our trust

It takes hard work throughout the years

and sometimes cost us many tears

The day will come when we'll set them free

praying that they've learned responsibility

When they have kids, it'll be so grand

then they will truly understand

Willie J. Pless III

There are rules and laws we must obey

as we go through life each day

So train your children and give it your best

one day they will be put to the test

Andrea Pless

Willie J. Pless III

Don't Worry

Life is full of problems

Each of us has his share

No matter who or what we are

It's something we all must bear

As I go through life each day

I fear that there may be

Temptation, trials, and troubles

waiting ahead of me

Some days can be a disaster

others are pretty good

Sometimes things just don't work out

the way I think they should

Willie J. Pless III

When problems seem get me down

it makes me realize

I have a lot to be thankful for

and then, to my surprise

My day gets a little brighter

I scurry along the way

I lift my head, take a deep breath

and thank God for another day

Don't Worry

Willie J. Pless III

A Real Friend

What is a friend and how do you know

if the friendship is true?

A friend is always willing to help

requiring nothing from you

A real friend is hard to find

and special in every way

A friend brings joy to those he meets

and brightens up their day

To be a friend is a greater reward

It's a very good feeling too

Willie J. Pless III

Knowing that someone needed help

and the friend that helped was you

Willie J. Pless III

Pless' Great grandfather & grandmother

Pop Todd & Mag Todd

Willie J. Pless III

Troubles

Trouble comes to everyone

On that we can depend

It enters our lives and lingers awhile

and one day, comes to an end

Trouble can be defeated

but, we cannot do it alone

It's God on whom we must depend

the one that sits on the throne

He'll take our troubles and work them out

and do it in his own way

The only thing required of us

is to trust in him and pray

Willie J. Pless III

When trouble comes our way again

Whatever its disguise

It makes us feel that we're all alone

But it's one more of the devil's lies

God is always with us

He knows our every care

Take your troubles to the Lord

Have faith and leave them there

Willie J. Pless III

Sorrow

Sorrow is something we all must bear

It's a part of life and will always be there

Sorrow comes in many ways

It steals our joy and darkens our days

Like everything else, it won't last long

It's here today, tomorrow it's gone

Enjoy your life and go about your way

For sorrow will return someday

And when it does, have no fear

Always remember that God is near

Willie J. Pless III

Willie J. Pless III

Faith

Troubles comes to everyone

On that you can depend

It enters our lives and lingers a while

And one day it comes to an end

If you haven't experienced trouble

You will one day, for sure

When trouble does come your way

It's very hard to endure

Trouble can be defeated

But we cannot do it alone

It's God on whom we must depend

The one that sits on the throne

                    Willie J. Pless III

He'll take our troubles and work them out

And, he'll do it in his way

The only thing required of us

Is to trust in him and pray

When troubles comes our way again

whatever maybe it's guise

It makes us feel like we're alone

but it's one more of the Devil's lies

Jesus is our comforter

he knows our every care

take your troubles to the Lord

Have faith and leave them there

Willie J. Pless III

Sickness

Sickness comes to every one

And usually there is a cure

But one thing you can count on

It will come one day for sure

Sickness came to me one day

And caught me off my guard

The doctors gave no relief

So I called upon the Lord

"Hello my son"

God said to me

What would you like me to do?

Forgive my sins and heal me Lord

That's what I need from you

Willie J. Pless III

And, from this day forward

This is what I'll do

I serve you Lord and spread your word

That others may follow you too

Willie J. Pless III

LOVE

LOVE is an important part of life

It's honest and it's fair

When you're alone and troubled

Love says "I care"

Love will never cheat

And love never lies

If a mistake has been made

Love will apologize

SHOW SOME LOVE!

Willie J. Pless III

Children

We bring our children into the world

and with them comes a chore

to love, train and protect

as our parents did before

Children learn from what they see

they'll do what others do

Willie J. Pless III

If we should do UNGODLY things

our children will do them too

When a child comes into this world

it brings us quite a joy

We pour out love and affection

be it girl or boy

As parents, we are responsible

for the things our children do

So train your children and train them well

their lives depend on you

Willie J. Pless III

Grand-daddy's Little Girls

Amara (top)

&

Mylan (bottom)

Willie J. Pless III

Heaven

I gaze upon the stars each night

some are dim, others quite bright

I often wonder as I stare

what's it like to be up there

I imagine that's how heaven will be

beauty, as far as the eye can see

There'll be no pain, and no more tears

just love and joy for infinite years

Willie J. Pless III

And when my life on earth is done

to my Lord, I will run

If anyone ask or look for me

tell them heaven is where I'll be

Willie J. Pless III

Trust

If someone puts his trust in you

and trust you as a friend

would you guard that person's trust

'til the very end?

Trust is a very delicate thing

It must be handled with care

Once the trust is broken

it's usually beyond repair

Even when friendship is restored

and the relationship regained

There will always be that cloud of doubt

and things won't be the same

Willie J. Pless III

Life can be hard sometimes

and everyone needs a friend

A friend in whom you can put your trust

and will keep it to the very end

If you need someone to trust

who's caring, honest, and fair

put your trust in the Lord

he'll treat it with loving care

Willie J. Pless III

Peace

As I look around the world each day

this is what I see

Wars, disasters, crime, hate

and immorality

How much longer can this go on

I ask myself each day

Things aren't getting any better

can we find a way?

I'm looking for something called peace

and now I can see

If it really doesn't exist

then it must begin with me

Now I have the answer

Willie J. Pless III

At least that's a start

but it's no good

unless it's understood

we all must do our part

Willie J. Pless III

Life

Sometimes life is hard to bear

even when you do your best

It makes us wonder, what have we done

to get in such a mess

Today could be a disaster

with no relief in sight

then you'll find to your surprise

you've made it through the night

Each day is a new day

we don't know what it will bring

It could bring something brand new

or maybe the same old thing

Willie J. Pless III

No matter what each day may bring

give it your very best

once you've done all you can

God will handle the rest

Willie J. Pless III

BOYS TO MEN

Willie J. Pless III

One day at a time

We go to bed each night,

after day is done

expecting to awake again

to see the rising sun

Many will see another day,

some won't make it through

We never know who's going to be

in the unfortunate few

Lord, thank you for another day,

you've been merciful and so kind

And as I continue on my way,

I'll take it one day at a time

Willie J. Pless III

All in the Family

Willie J. Pless III

Broken Heart

A broken heart will come one day

unwanted, uninvited, unfair

It comes for many reasons

and seems impossible to bear

Day by day it lingers

clinging like a vine

One day it'll be over

but it takes a little time

Meanwhile, trust and believe in God

On him we can depend

Friends and family may let you down

but God is there 'til the end

Willie J. Pless III

The Road of Life

I travel this old road each day

trying to stay on track

I carefully plan and chart my path

to keep from sliding back

No matter how perfect my plan may be

there's always the unknown

It is then I am reminded

that I cannot do it alone

As I continue on my journey

off the path, I may stray

That is when I call on the Lord

for he will show me the way

Willie J. Pless III

It's A Family Affair

Willie J. Pless III

Famliy Ties

Willie J. Pless III

Hard Times

I often sit in silent throughts

of many years gone by

Some were filled with joy

others made me cry

Days of sadness and sorrow

brought with them many tears

The burden continued on and on

over the passing years

One day God knocked at my door

I gladly let him in

He said he came to ease my pain

and wash away my sins

God told me things that I must do

while in this earthly life

To brake the chains that bound me

Willie J. Pless III

with misery, pain and strife

He said that I must trust in him

to get me through each day

I must believe and follow him

For that's the only way

Willie J. Pless III

Family Portrait

Willie J. Pless III

Willie J. Pless III

ABOUT THE POET

Willie J Pless III is 63, and he's the oldest of eight siblings. He graduated from Howard High School in 1967 and proceeded to attend DeKalb Tech. There he obtained a certification in small engine repair, small appliance repair, and basic electrical repair.

He retired from Ga. Power Co. after 29 years and later retired from the YMCA. He has been married to his wife Jacque for 27 years. He has two sons and two daughters and eight grand children each child has two children.

He dedicated his life to JESUS at a very early age. He is a member of House of Prayer Christian Church where he serves as a Deacon.

Willie J. Pless III

He loved to quote his own poetry so he began to write them down and later his wife had them copy written.

In 2004 he was diagnosed with Dementia.

In present time his dementia has progressed but, yet he still remembers that he wants to do something with his poems.

Willie J. Pless III

Willie J. Pless III

Printed by Libri Plureos GmbH in Hamburg, Germany